THE
MAWDDACH ESTUARY

by

W. HOWEL EVANS M.D. F.R.S.A.

and

MAIR JONES LLB. (Hons)

First published 1996 by Countyvise Limited, 1 & 3 Grove Road, Rock Ferry, Birkenhead, Wirral, Merseyside L42 3XS.

Copyright © 1996

ISBN 0 907768 91 1

All rights reserved. No part of this publication may be reproduced, stored in a retrieval system, or transmitted, in any form, or by any means, electronic, chemical, mechanical, photocopying, recording or otherwise, without the prior permission of the publisher.

The Brigantine 'Charlotte' built at Llyn Penmaen (Penmaenpool) in 1862.

CONTENTS

Pages	
1	Llanelltyd
3	Cymer Abbey
4	Chalice and Paten
5	Dolgellau
8	Maesygarnedd
10	Penmaenpool
11	Arthog
14	Fairbourne and Friog
15	Cader Idris
18	Bontddu and Gwynfynydd
20	Barmouth (Abermaw)

ILLUSTRATIONS

The Brigantine 'Charlotte'   (Frontispiece)
Llanelltyd Bridge
Cader Range and Arfon Mawddach
from east of LLanelltyd
Cymer Abbey
Chalice and Paten
Dolgellau from the bridge
The Mawddach from Dolgellau Golf Club
Penmaenpool - the spur leading to the Estuary
Penmaenpool - the George III Hotel
Upper Arthog to estuary and Lleyn Peninsula
The Beach at Fairbourne facing Friog
Cader Iris from Llanelltyd
Cader Iris and Afon Mawddach from near Bontddu
Outlet of Mawddach at low tide from Fairbourne
Barmouth from Penrhyn Point
The Round House, Barmouth
Barmouth bridge looking up estuary
Harbour at Barmouth
Coes Faen - prominent landmark on estuary, on road
out of Barmouth towards Dolgellau

INTRODUCTION

The Mawddach Estuary is justly famous as one of the most beautiful spots in the British Isles. It is situated in the southern aspect of the Snowdonia National Park in Gwynedd, formerly Merionethshire. It is largely unspoilt and, surprisingly, is not widely known.

The Mawddach Estuary lies between the River Glaslyn to the north and the River Dovey to the south and all these flow into Cardigan Bay.

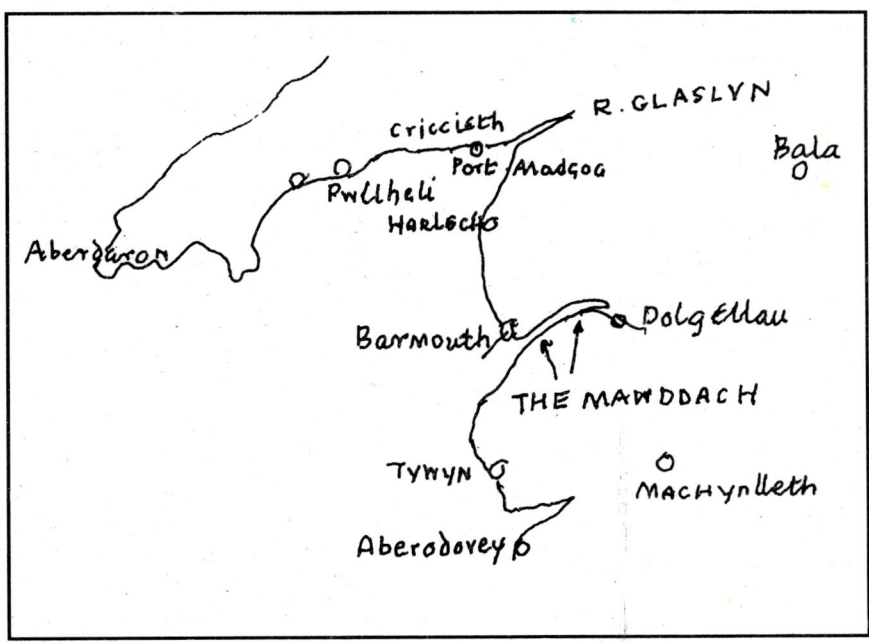

The Mawddach is one of the best known rivers in the Snowdownia National Park and it is six miles long. It rises north, in the cotton grass moors east of Duallt and enters the estuary at Llanelltyd.

The aim of this book is to follow the course of the River Mawddach from east to west with short descriptions and some history of the various points. These will be illustrated with original watercolours, photographs or prints.

The areas illustrated will be as follows

1. Llanelltyd
2. Cymer Abbey
3. Dolgellau
4. Maesygarnedd
5. Penmaenpool
6. Arthog
7. Fairbourne and Friog
8. Cader Idris
9. Bontddu and Gwynfynydd
10. Barmouth

LLANELLTYD

Llanelltyd Bridge

    This village is two miles from Dolgellau on the northern side of the Mawddach. It has a turn-pike house where the road branches, one way leading to Barmouth, the other to the east towards the Ganllwyd valley. It overlooks the Llanelltyd bridge which crosses the Mawddach and this arched stone bridge is no longer used by traffic as a new bridge has been built a short distance down the river to the west, but it can be crossed on foot. The River Mawddach ceases to be tidal at the point where the old bridge crosses it.

    The church at Llanelltyd, dedicated to St. Illtyd, was built in 1291 and when the Cistercian monks came to Cymer Abbey they served the church for three and a half centuries. The church is a delightful example of mediaeval Celtic architecture. It has a very distinctive feature for it stands in the middle of a circular graveyard. Historically, the altar was a very holy place and anyone who claimed sanctuary of the altar was protected. A circle was drawn round the altar by a ploughman and his team of oxen and, so long as the person remained within the circle, he could claim sanctuary for seven years and seven days. The main entrance to the church is on the Dolgellau to Trawsfynydd road and is believed to date from the end of the 18th century. The old entrance was on the south west, connected to the road by a flight of stone steps. The old door and porch can still be seen.

In 1876 an old stone was found near the church bearing the imprint of a foot and a Latin inscription. This has been translated as "the footprint of Cynwrig is imprinted on the head of this stone before he set off on a pilgrimage to foreign parts." One theory for the placing of the foot on the stone was that the pilgrim considered that it was a guarantee of a safe return from his pilgrimage.

Between the church and the river stands a house called Ty'n Llan which was at one time an inn patronised by miners working in the nearby gold mines of the Mawddach valley, and it was also a place for worshippers to stable their horses during church services.

Cader Idris and Afon Mawddach from east of Llanelltyd

CYMER ABBEY

In 1198 monks came to lay the foundations of a Cistercian abbey, which was dedicated to the Virgin Mary, as was Dolgellau Parish Church. The Abbey lies in beautiful countryside on the eastern side of the Mawddach near Llanelltyd bridge. There was good access to the estuary, the valley of the River Wnion, the valley of Ganllwyd and the main thoroughfare to Llanelltyd. This was the only monastery in Merioneth at the time of the Reformation and it had considerable influence over a wide area for several centuries. In 1209 it was given a Charter which gave it possession to estates stretching from Barmouth and inland beyond Dolgellau.

There was no bridge over the Mawddach and often travellers would have to spend the night on the river bank when the river was running high and unsafe to cross. Here one of the facilities of the Abbey was to provide a resting place for the travellers.

The Mawddach Estuary

After the Charter of 1209, the Abbey had three dependent churches in Llanelltyd, Llanfachreth and Llanegryn. The Cistercians were well known for their services to agriculture and, although they did not cultivate on an extensive scale, they did carry on a considerable trade in wool. The Abbey was adjacent to a good fishing pool and the monks were confirmed in the use of this pool by the Charter of 1209. This was very valuable to the monks and provided more than their needs.

The fate of the Abbey was to come in 1536 when Henry the Eighth passed an Act dissolving those monasteries whose revenues did not exceed £200 per year. Cymer's revenue yielded only £51.13.4 per year and therefore it was dissolved.

The magnificent rood screen from the Abbey was placed in Llanegryn Church, where it can still be seen.

THE CHALICE AND PATEN

The chalice and paten were found in 1890 by two men when they were prospecting for gold on the mountain side a few miles from Llanelltyd. The significance of the find was not realised until later and then they were recognised as two examples of late thirteenth century church plate. Experts are sure that they were made of silver gilt and that they were made in Westphalia in Germany. It has been popularly suggested that the chalice and paten came from Cymer Abbey, but now the association is regarded as conjectural. They are now housed in the National Museum of Wales, Cardiff.

(By permission of The National Museum of Wales)

DOLGELLAU

Dolgellau originated as a village in the twelfth and thirteenth centuries and the town is situated in beautiful countryside at the foot of Cader Idris. The severe stone architectural style of the town blends well with the rugged surrounding landscape. The layout of the town is of interest, being based on a series of small squares linked by narrow streets.

The seven-arched bridge which crosses the River Wnion was originally built in 1638, but alterations have been made since then as a result of changes in forms of transport and flood damage. The County Hall is situated at the foot of the bridge and this is where the Assizes were held until discontinued. The County Court and the local Magistrates' Court still hold regular sessions there.

Dolgellau from the bridge

There are traces of Roman remains by Ffynnon Mair (Mary's Spring) which was famous for its healing properties. Some Roman coins of the Emperors Hadrian and Trajan were found nearby about two centuries ago, and they were thought to have been dropped by Roman soldiers. Owain Glyndwr's Parliament House stood on a site now occupied by an ironmonger's store and it was here that he held his Council of Chiefs in the fifteenth century.

There is evidence of a church on the site of the present Parish Church of St. Mary since the twelfth contury. The old church was demolished and the present church built in 1716. Its main feature is the massive oak pillars which support the roof. They are said to have been pulled by oxen over Bwlch yr Oerddrws, the steep pass between Dinas Mawddwy and Dolgellau. By tradition, the bells ring a curfew at 9pm as in mediaeval times.

The district around Dolgellau is closely associated with Quakers where the cause was established in 1657 and its followers suffered persecution for their faith. In 1686 Rowland Elis, a prominent local Quaker who lived in Bryn Mawr on the lower slopes of Cader range, emigrated to Pennsylvania and there was to found the famous women's college of Bryn Mawr. In our own times (1991) "Ty Meirion," a Quaker centre, was established in Eldon Square in the centre of the town and this provides an interesting link with the notable associations mentioned. It is of interest that Yale University was also founded by a Welshman, Ellhi Ial from Denbighshire.

The Dolgellau Grammar School for Boys was one of the earliest grammar schools in Wales, endowed by Dr. John Ellis, Rector of Dolgellau, in 1665. The teaching staff had to be graduates of either Oxford or Cambridge. The old school building was demolished in 1969, but the school itself had moved to larger premises before the beginning of this century. The present school, Ysgol y Gader, is co-educational.

Dr. Williams' School for Girls was founded in 1878 under the origins of an educational trust established by the will of Dr. Daniel Williams. It was an independent school and it attracted pupils from all parts of the United Kingdom and beyond. It was closed in 1975.

Dolgellau was famous for establishing the wool trade. It was said at the time that "nearly every poor man had his own loom wheron he made his 'webs' to support his family." The webs were made up into bales or half bales. In the eighteenth and nineteenth centuries,

The Mawddach Estuary

Dolgellau was the centre of the Merioneth woollen industry and the products were carried down the River Wnion and then transferred to the River Mawddach for transporting to the port of Barmouth for forward shipping. The local Rotary Club has revived this tradition and an annual Wool Race is held where bales of wool are carried by raft down the River Mawddach by competing teams. There are remains of the woollen mills on the outskirts of the town and it is only in the last few years that the local tannery has closed. Here the bales of wool, collected from local farms, were treated and transported to Yorkshire for manufacturing into cloth.

Dolgellau attracts visitors from all over the world, especially at holiday times. It is ideally suited for walkers with a wide choice of climbs and rambles. Fishermen are also well catered for and golfers could easily be distracted by the glorious views of the Mawddach estuary seen from Dolgellau Golf Club. (see plate 4). An excellent walk is the one along the disused railway track from Dolgellau and up to Morfa Mawddach on the south side of the Barmouth railway bridge and viaduct which has been converted to a nature walk. Between Penmaenpool and Arthog, the path runs alongside the banks of the

The Mawddach from Dolgellau Golf Club

The Mawddach Estuary

Mawddach estuary giving the walker another aspect of the beauty of the area and it is also a good vantage point to see the many species of sea birds and ducks.

The Marian, a large expanse of meadow skirted by the River Wnion, is home to the Dolgellau Cricket Club, which was established in the nineteenth century and, more recently, to the Rugby Union club. Adjoining the Cricket Club pavilion there is a circle of large, rough-hewn stones erected when the National Eisteddfod of Wales was held in the town in 1949. At the far end of the Marian car park is the Welsh Gold Centre, a new development for the town. Here you can see rare Welsh gold from the nearby Gwynfynydd Gold Mines being worked into jewellery and visits to the mine can be made daily.

During the nineteenth century printing was an important industry in Dolgellau and the earliest press started in 1798. The old method of hot pressing was used to print the local newspaper Y Dydd (The Day) which was first published in 1868, but nowadays modern technology has taken over.

The Welsh language is spoken by a majority of the inhabitants of Dolgellau and Welsh cultural traditions hold an important part in the life of the town.

MAESYGARNEDD

This small creek is a stone's throw from Llanelltyd and 6 miles from Barmouth. It was a busy ship-building centre and also a trading centre for the distribution for goods and merchandise from Barmouth for local residents and those further afield. The merchandise consisted of flour, oatmeal, beans, rye, wheat, rice, powder, soap, candles, salt, coal, timber, skins, bark and wine.

The Mawddach Estuary

Penaenpool

PENMAENPOOL (LLYN PENMAEN)

Two or three miles from Dolgellau on the Towyn road stands Penmaenpool. It is on an inlet where the Mawddach takes a course inland; it is a very picturesque spot. An hotel stands on the bank of the estuary and it is known now as the George III. It was built in 1650 in two separate buildings, one half a pub, the other a ship-builders. The boats were often large (see frontispiece). They were towed across to Barmouth by rowing boats for completing with sails, rigging etc. The amount of shipping during the eighteenth and nineteenth centuries was considerable but it virtually ceased with the arrival of the railways. The two buildings were then joined into one to make the existing hotel and the shipyard was closed. In the meantime, the Cambrian Railway opened a railway which passes directly through Penmaenpool and even level with the hotel. However, in 1964 the line was closed by Dr. Beeching's cuts and all that remains is a signal. The former signal box is a bird-watcher's observation point. A tollbridge lies adjacent to the hotel and this crosses the estuary to join the Barmouth road on the opposite bank. It was built of wood in 1879 and was capable of conversion for the passage of ships should shipbuilding return to Maesygarnedd.

Penaenpool

ARTHOG

The village of Arthog straddles the road from Dolgellau to Tywyn. The name is thought to derive from a personal name, Arthawg. The large house up on the hillside is known as Arthog Hall, but was formerly known as Pwllarthog (pwll means pit in Welsh).

The road from Dolgellau passes the remains of Arthog's industrial past - slate quarrying - which started up in the mid 1860s. The excavated galleries of Ty'n y Coed quarry can be seen on the left hand side of the road and the finished slates were carried by tramway, (the remains of the bridge can be seen today) to a small jetty on the banks of the Mawddach far below, where they were loaded on to boats to be taken to Barmouth. After the Aberystwyth and West Coast railway was opened from Penmaenpool to Aberdovey, the slates were thereafter transported by rail. The quarry closed in the 1880s as competition from the quarries at Corris and Ffestiniog made it uneconomic.

Following the road down the hill, the old National School with bell tower - dated 1844 - is on the left and leads to a narrow single arch stone bridge and further on the right, the church.

Opposite the church is an old mill and water from Arthog stream was channelled to work the waterwheel. The mill stones are still on the site.

Driving through the village there are small terraces of houses. Arthog Terrace, was built around the 1860s and its well-kept gardens are situated across the road. One small house, Pencei, meaning 'end of quay' still exists. Before the embankments were built, high tides came up to the turnpike and probably small boats could travel up the channel to load at Pencei quay.

On a sandy bay on the banks of the Mawddach is an impressive row of houses, Mawddach Crescent. This was erected by Solomon Andrews, a Cardiff business man who was so impressed by the beauty of the district around Arthog that he bought several local farms and later built three terraces of houses. Situated above the road is Afon y Morfa, at one time a small farm whose original buildings were thought to date from the seventeenth century.

John Price, who was a tenant some time in the nineteenth century, also owned a boat in which he carried peat to Barmouth. A vast quantity of peat was cut on the Arthog bog which was then dried and loaded at the stone quay on the Mawddach to be carried to Barmouth by river, before the advent of the railway. Arthog bog still provides the botanist with examples of interesting species of plants. Another quarry was opened in the mid 1860s - Tyddyn Sieffre - but this venture foundered and the company went into liquidation.

The Cyfanedd Fawr silver-lead mine was the only mine in the district. Lead ore collected from the mine was taken by ferry to Barmouth and then shipped to Swansea for smelting and refining. One assay produced 40 oz. silver to one ton of ore.

The oldest man in the district, David Evans, farmed actively up to the age of 99 when he retired and lived to the age of 103. He was of a generation who worked hard all their lives in difficult conditions and this exemplifies the longevity of many others, men and women, living in this area.

There is a Quaker burial ground in nearby Llwyngwril and traces of a grave have been found in land in Arthog at Cynfanedd Ucha.

A narrow steep road leads from Arthog up to the Cregennan Lakes, a noted beauty spot, and the subject of many paintings and photographs. The road skirts the lakes and joins the road leading

Estuary from Arthog

down to Dolgellau. At one time there was a small settlement of people living in Cregennan but latterly many of the houses have fallen into disrepair.

Another interesting Arthog connection is the Nannau Bronze Bucket, which was found by children at Nannau, near Dolgellau, and acquired by the National Museum of Wales in 1965. The bucket was made of thin bronze sheets riveted together with a circular handle on each side of the rim and was of the 'Kurdish' type, originating from Central Eastern Europe. It was recorded that an identical bucket was found at Ty'n y Coed and it is considered that it found its way to Nannau, where it was rediscovered.

There is evidence of human activity in the district going back probably to the Bronze Age by virtue of finds of implements used and the distinctive methods of burials adopted. A number of large, flat stones were placed on edge to form a cist in which the body remains were placed. A large stone covered the cist which was subsequently covered by a mound of stones. Some cists measured 50 feet and one of the largest found locally was opened in 1851. The number of cists remaining have been reduced as stones have been taken to build walls.

One of the cists was a vessel with a stone over its mouth, containing remains. This identifies the burial as by the 'Beaker Folk' who came over from the Continent at the end of the third and the beginning of the second Millenium BC. They got their name from this practice of placing remains in a beaker or urn.

Other reminders of Bronze Age people have been found in the form of weapons or implements. One was a palstave, an early form of axe, attributed to the Middle Bronze Age around 1500 to 1000 BC. Another, a socketed axe, of approximately 1000 to 500 BC was found, as was also a stone axe hammer. These finds show that as long ago as 3000 BC travellers were moving through the area, if not living there.

The Beach at Fairbourne facing Friog

FAIRBOURNE AND FRIOG

Fairbourne is a pleasant seaside resort and has been since Victorian times. The village consists of an arcade of shops, several large houses, holiday houses, bungalows, many of recent origin, and some small caravan and camping sites. There is a safe, sandy beach over two miles long which is very popular for bathing and windsurfing. The local church, St. Cynons, was consecrated in 1927.

The Cambrian Coast railway, part of British Rail, runs across the long railway bridge from Barmouth, thence through Fairbourne to Llwyngwril and Tywyn. Fairbourne is however famous for its other railway, the Fairbourne narrow gauge railway, a very popular attraction for holiday makers. It runs through the village and alongside the sea shore to Penrhyn Point. From this sandy peninsula the views up the Mawddach are truly spectacular with mountain ranges on either side. From Penrhyn Point, passengers can embark on a ferry to Barmouth harbour on the opposite side of the estuary. It is believed that the franchise to the ferry was granted in the reign of Edward I and it is

THE MAWDDACH ESTUARY

mentioned in 1565. The island at the mouth of the river is known as Ynys y Brawd - Friar's Island - which raises speculation that the ferry was originally run by a religious order.

The western end of the Cader Range overlooks Friog which lies about one mile from Fairboune along the main road from Dolgellau to Tywyn. The Non-conformist chapels and some boarding houses are situated here. At the far end of Friog, where a minor road leads to the beach, there is a Toll house.

Above Friog lie the Panteinion Falls and the Blue Lake, which is on the land of the Friog Slate Quarry.

CADER IDRIS

The Cader range has true mountain qualities with precipices dropping almost sheer to deep lakes: it has a fine high summit ridge, with screes, boulders and high wet gullies where alpine plants are found. Snow lies, at least patchily, on its northern face for many months from late autumn to spring. (Condry 1973)

Cader Idris stands at the highest peak of the Cader range (2927 feet) and there are several mountains in South Merioneth which almost reach the 3000 feet mark, the highest being Aran Mawddwy (2970 feet).

The views from Cader Idris in fine weather are magnificent, - to the north, Snowdon, the Arenig Mountains and the Arans to the east, and westward the beauty of the Mawddach, leading to Cardigan Bay, and south, the Dysyni valley and in the far distance, Pembrokeshire. On a clear day the Wicklow Mountains of Ireland can be seen. There are a number of routes to the summit of Cader Idris, some being more taxing than others.

The origin of the name Cader Idris is shrouded in mythology. Some say that Idris was a giant and the name literally means 'the Chair of Idris.'

Legend has it that anyone sleeping on the mountain overnight will awake either as a madman or a poet.

The Mawddach Estuary

Cader Idris from Llanelltyd

THE MAWDDACH ESTUARY

Cader Idris and Mawddach fom Bontddu

BONTDDU AND GWYNFYNYDD

THE GOLD MINES

The village of Bontddu lies on the Barmouth to Dolgellau road on the north bank of the Mawddach. The church at Caerdeon is on the outskirts of the village and its unusual design blends perfectly with its wooded surroundings.

Above the village on the road to the Diffwys mountain lies the Clogau gold mine. Some of the gold mines of Wales are to be found in the Mawddach valley and are situated along the northern and western slopes of the valley from Bontddu. It has been suggested that the Welsh gold mines have been worked intermittently from the times of the Romans, but there is no evidence of this in this particular locality. However, the monks of Cymer Abbey were given 'the right in digging or carrying away metals and treasures...' Mining for gold in the area began in the 1840s when a number of small mines was established. The gold was found in quartz veins, in which there were also quantities of silver, iron, copper and other metals. In Gwynfynydd, in particular, the quartz veins were found deep within the mountain. By the end of the 1860s, the first 'gold rush' was virtually over, but in 1888 a new find at Gwynfynydd re-opened the workings.

The main mines were the Clogau, situated in the hills overlooking the Mawddach estuary, and the Gwynfynydd mine in the Coed-y-Brenin forest in the Ganllwyd valley, north of Dolgellau. In the processing of the gold, a certain amount of it was lost and carried down the River Mawddach and this may explain why quantities of alluvial gold have been found from time to time in the Mawddach estuary between Llanelltyd and Penmaenpool. The Clogau mine was closed down in 1910 but has been re-opened many times since. However, it has not produced enough gold for it to be an economic proposition.

The Gwynfynydd mine has been re-opened within the last decade and a considerable amount of gold has been extracted. The mine is an attraction to tourists visiting the area and conducted tours of the mines to see the workings are available. In the Welsh Gold Centre situated in the Marian car park in Dolgellau, visitors can see and purchase jewellery made from gold from the Gwynfyndd mine.

By tradition, Royal wedding rings have been made from the rare, pure Welsh gold found in the mines of the Mawddach and Ganllwyd valleys.

The Mawddach Estuary

Outlet of the Mawddach at Fairbourne Point.

Barmouth from Penryhn Point, Fairbourne

BARMOUTH

Barmouth was originally a tiny hamlet with four houses, according to 'A Return of Harbours and Creeks in Merioneth' published in 1565 in the reign of Elizabeth I. The name, Barmouth, is probably a corruption of Abermawddach or Bermo. It is in the parish of St. Mary's in Llanaber, an ancient twelfth century Anglican church.

Little is known until the early seventeenth century when trading by sea to the south and to the north became important and wool was the main cargo, but the Civil War disrupted this trading and the town remained poor and backward. However, in 1750 at least 15 sloops were built on the river Mawddach and Barmouth became the chief harbour of Merioneth.

Subsequently the trade was woollen goods, mainly cloth and stockings. Imports continued with foodstuffs, household goods, spirits etc. and exports included woollen goods, oakbark timber, cheese and butter. Since 1766 Barmouth has been a sea bathing resort and this seasonal trade established the town's prosperity in the second half of the eighteenth century, when bathing in the sea had become a fashion. Barmouth has a fine sandy beach, mountain views, river walks, convivial company and low tariffs.

Women, however, had to use bathing machines 'for the sake of propriety.' Links were established between visitors and the local people. There was a good supply of accommodation and the inn keepers were often women. Some notable visitors came to Barmouth in the nineteenth century, including the poets, Shelley, Wordsworth, Ruskin, Tennyson and also Darwin and Gladstone.

In 1830 there were drunken riots in the town and meetings were held as to how to control them. A Round House was built and opened in 1834 and it is still one of the historic features of Barmouth. It was used until 1861 when a police station was opened in Barmouth. It then fell into a state of disrepair but has now been restored. It is situated on sand dunes between the promenade and St. David's church and is a circular stone structure with a pitched slate roof and it has a centre shaft with the appearance of a chimney. The building was divided into two cells of equal size by a partition wall two feet thick. The cells have high, narrow openings to provide light and ventilation

Round House

The Mawddach Estuary

Barmouth Bridge - looking up Estuary - Cader range in background

with an external door to each cell. One cell was for men and one for women. The Round House was used as a lock-up to detain drunkards until they became sober and was also used for holding an accused person pending his or her transfer to a place "where justice could be administered." Barmouth was a flourishing sea-port in the eighteenth and early nineteenth centuries, used by both British and foreign ships and it was probable that there was a need for a safe place to contain the rowdy elements of both sexes.

Apart from the seasonal trade, goods were not found in shops until the nineteenth century, when items such as shoes would be bought from workshops. Itinerant fishermen would bring their catch to be sold at the quayside.

The Non-conformists had established themselves in the latter half of the eighteenth century. Their influence had a sobering effect on the community by their exercise of thrift and self-discipline.

The original church of St. Mary's, Llanaber, became too small to meet the needs of the population and in 1830, another Anglican church, St. David's, was built on the site of a ship-building yard in the harbour area of the town. As the town was expanding to the north west and the population was growing, another larger Anglican church was built overlooking the town and St. John's church was opened in 1892. The foundation stone had been laid by Princess Beatrice, the daughter of Queen Victoria.

By 1867, Barmouth had developed into a small town rather than a fishing or sea-faring village. In the season, the population grew to 1,733 in 1871, but the railway was to have an immediate effect on shipping. Slate was now being carried by rail and, although Barmouth, Pwllheli and Caernarvon were still exporting slate in 1830, the trade declined.

The demise of the slate trade was a severe blow to all the ports in Caernarvonshire and Merionethshire. The goods which entered Barmouth harbour were destined for customers in Dolgellau and surrounding districts and Penmaenpool, Maesgarnedd and Llanelltyd had provision for unloading cargoes from small boats. However, the approach to Barmouth harbour could be dangerous, and there were as many as 22 shipwrecks in the area. The local life-boat saved many lives and the history of the Barmouth life-boat is depicted in the Royal National Lifeboat Institution Museum in the port area.

The Mawddach Estuary

The harbour at Barmouth

Barmouth bridge is a very distinctive feature of the Mawddach estuary. It was built in 1867 to bring the railway into Barmouth. The footpath runs along the rail track and allows spectacular views of the estuary. Part of the bridge, nearest to Barmouth, is designed to swing open to allow tall-masted ships to pass through.

Barmouth has a unique connection with the National Trust which was established in March 1895. The first gift to the Trust was donated by Mrs. Fanny Talbot, a Barmouth resident. It was an area of land four and a half acres in size, known as Dinas Oleu, a gorse covered headland of wild flowers and pathways overlooking the Mawddach Estuary, with views of Cader Idris, Cardigan Bay and the Lleyn peninsula.

Barmouth boasts a mediaeval building in the centre of the town, known as Ty Gwyn. It is reputed to have been built by Gruffydd Fechan of Cors y Gedol in the fifteenth century as a safe meeting place to plan an invasion of Britain; it is now a museum.

The Mawddach Estuary

Barmouth has had many vicissitudes in the past, as the reader will gather from this text. That they have largely surmounted them is a fact. This is due, in large part, to the resolution of the citizens of Barmouth. The seasonal holiday-makers remain loyal to the town - an important influence to the town's economy. Fishing has recently been started again which should add to its prosperity - long may it last!

Coes Faen - prominent landmark on estuary, on road out of Barmouth towards Dolgellau

ACKNOWLEDGEMENTS

We should like to thank -

Dr. Brynley Roberts, Librarian, the National Library of Wales, for references and access to the Library and his help and encouragement.

William Condry for his valuable and comprehensive book on the Snowdonia National Park.

Mr. Ifor Higgon for his extensive study of Arthog.

And lastly, to Miss Mary Howel Evans for her help in typing from our original scripts.

REFERENCES

The Snowdonia National Park.	W. Condry 1973
Barmouth and Maritime Merionethshire	W. Lewis Lloyd 1973
Treasures of the Mawddach.	Hugh J. Owen 1950
A History of Barmouth and its vicinity.	E. Rosalie Jones 1909
'The Light of Other Days,' a history of Friog and Fairbourne.	Alison Harrison (no date)
Arthog	Ifor Higgon Unpublished (1990)
Dolgellau	A.M. and K.O. Rees 1972
The story of 2 parishes Dolgelley & Llanelltyd	T.P. Ellis 1928
Hanes Dolgellau	John Jones 1872